Copyright © 2021 by Eugene Mosley
Interior Illustrations by Johnny Davis of UCANTDRAW
Interior Illustrations © 2021 by Eugene Mosley

All rights reserved. Published by Malcom Explains, LLC
No part of this publication may be reproduced, stored in a retrieval system, or transmitted in any form or by any means, electronic, mechanical, photocopying, recording, or otherwise, without expressed written permission of the publisher. For information regarding permission, please write to Malcom Explains, LLC, Attention: Media Department, PO Box 18193, Shreveport, LA 71118.

ISBN-13: 978-1-7373508-6-6

Printed in the U.S.A.
First edition, November 2021

To My Father and Mother:
Mr. Huey P Mosley & Mrs. Barbara W. Mosley

To My Uncle:
Mr. Milton Rambo

To My Art Teacher:
Mr. Billy Adgers

And to all of the young artist in the world, keep your head up and follow your calling.

WRITTEN BY
UGENE MOSLEY

THE KID THAT ACCEPTED GOD'S CALLING

ILLUSTRATED BY
JOHNNY DAVIS OF
UCANTDRAW

THE EUGENE MOSLEY STORY

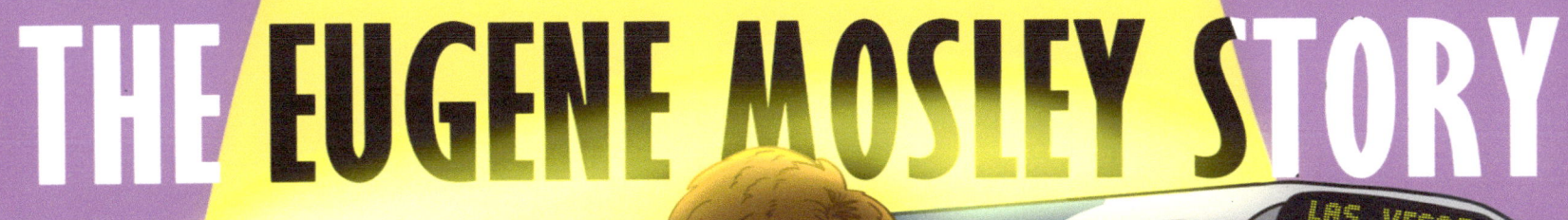

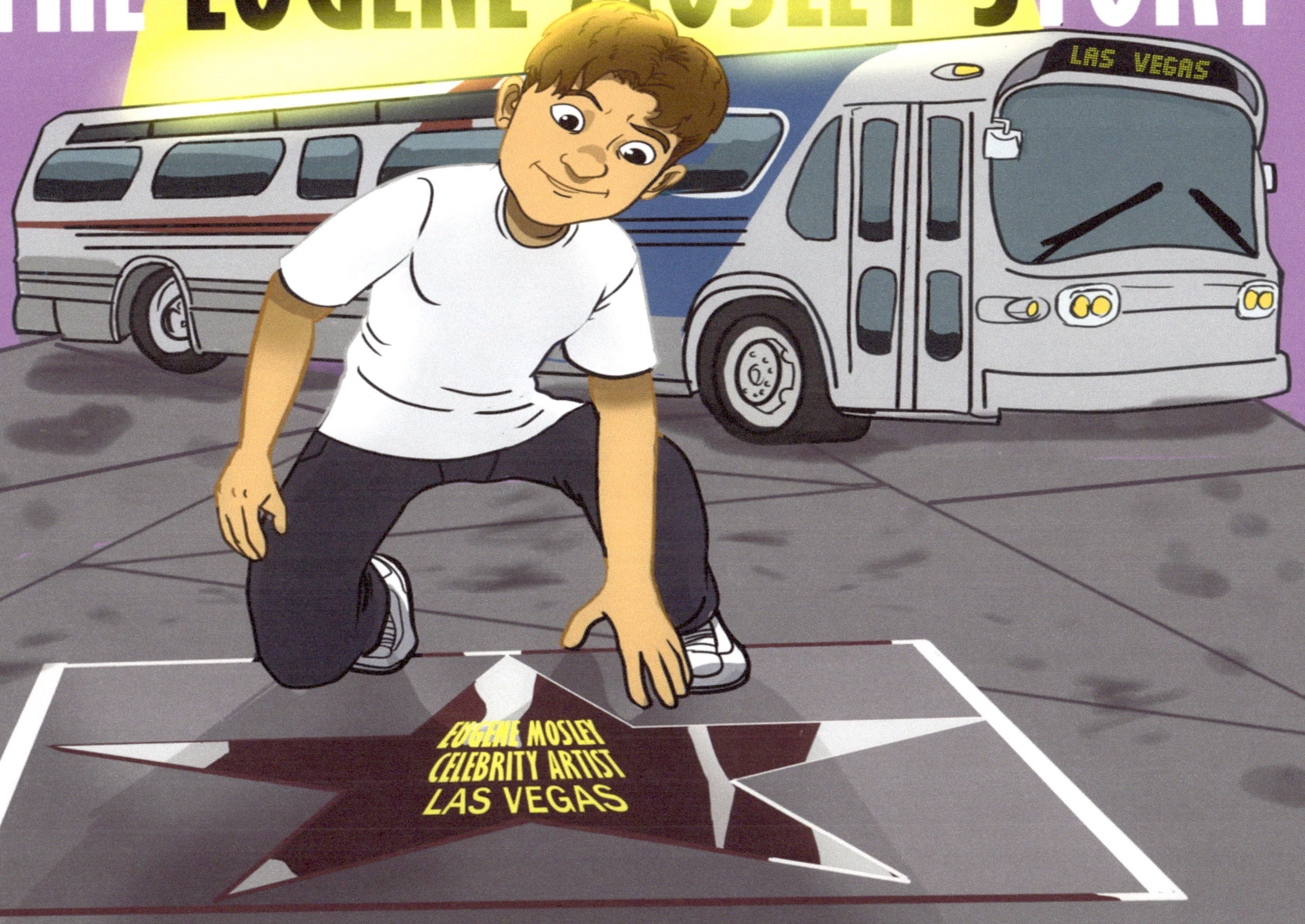

Eugene lived in this house, at 3823 Mayfield Street. It is located in a city called Shreveport, and a state called Louisiana. Louisiana is a state that is known for great food and music, especially jazz. It was in this house that little Eugene found out that his dreams can come true.

The day arrives for little Eugene to leave on a trip that will change his life, forever. His dad takes him to the Greyhound Bus Station. As they waited for the bus, over the sound system a loud voice says, *Las Vegas is leaving at Gate 7 in 10 minutes.* As Eugene entered the bus, his dad asks him for his seat number. He said, "Dad it is seat number 2."

His dad replies, "Okay, I love you son." Eugene responded back to his dad, "Love you too dad," with a scared voice. Seeing the worried look on Eugene's Dad's face, the bus driver told him that he would look out for his son. A sigh of relief could be seen on his dad's face as he waved goodbye to him at the door. And, off he went.

As the day goes by and night begins to set in, little Eugene falls asleep. Missing his family and not knowing what to expect the next day had him feeling scared. However, he did not need to worry because his Grandma and his Uncle Milton would be waiting for him.

After a long bus ride, little Eugene finally makes it to Las Vegas, Nevada. And, yes, his Uncle Milton was there to meet him. He was a tall man, wearing jeans, a white shirt, and a blue baseball cap. Little Eugene thought he was really cool looking. He was so happy to see him. Uncle Milton asked him how was his trip? He replied,

"It was great! Dad and mom are also doing great." Uncle Milton said with a smile on his face, "Okay, let's go to grandma's house. She is going to be so excited to see you."

After a long trip and talking to his Grandma Jewell and to his mom and dad on the phone, little Eugene was getting sleepy. So, he turned on the clock radio in his room to Radio Station 88.1 and they were playing Jazz music, which reminded him of home.

Although feeling very tired, he could not sleep because of the bright lights shining through his bedroom window - all night long.

As hours go by, little Eugene finally makes it to the Strip. He was getting very thirsty. As he passed a lot of big buildings, not knowing that they were called casinos, he decided to walk up to one named "The Sands" to get something to drink.

Little Eugene makes it inside the casino and gets some water from a nearby fountain. As he was walking back to the front entrance, he runs across a man drawing portraits of all kinds of sceneries.

Little Eugene thought to himself, "Wow, this looks so real and cool!" So, he stood behind him, just looking, in amazement as he was drawing.

Not knowing that his cousins were over for Sunday dinner and listening, he pours his heart out to his Grandma about what he wanted to be when he grows up. They started laughing and saying, "You need to stay away from the strip and stop that wishful dreaming." Little Eugene could see that his grandma was not pleased with what his cousins were doing and saying to him. So, she says, "Stop laughing at him."

Summer is over! Uncle Milton takes little Eugene to the bus station where he anxiously waits on the Greyhound bus heading back to Shreveport, Louisiana.

The Eugene Mosley Story

```
X W J P O I N T I L L I S M N
F J M R J S G R E Y H O U N D
Y A K W K T U S Q R D F R Q T
R Z I A F E O A O U E R J B J
E Z M L X V F M D W A A F G M
G M W K U E R M L J N N P R N
I U A O X H Y Y A J M K X A C
S S T F S A N D S C A S I N O
G I E S A R J A V J R I A D H
A C R T V V B V E N T N R M V
L O S A G E K I G X I A T A T
E H B R V Y R S A O N T I P V
R Z R S G J I X S H L R S U Q
I L S O U T H W O O D A T X Y
E Z D U K E E L L I N G T O N
```

Duke Ellington
Steve Harvey
Greyhound
Southwood

Frank Sinatra
Pointillism
Dean Martin
Las Vegas

Sands Casino
Regis Galerie
Sammy Davis
Grandma

Walk of Stars
Kim Waters
Jazz Music
Artist

As the years go by, Eugene really begins to notice that his mother loves to paint and that his dad is really a big jazz enthusiast. One morning, Eugene decides to tell his mom and dad something really important. His mother was painting and his dad was listening to his jazz music. However, both of them gave Eugene their full

attention as he proceeded to tell them about his big announcement. "Mom and dad, I know what I want to be when I grow up." His mom says, "What son?" He says, "I want to be a famous artist." His dad says, "Now, that's great son!" While his mom excitedly said to him, "You go for it! Now, when school starts, you need to take some art classes. You can do it, son."

Eugene now attends high school at Southwood High School. Determined to be a famous artist, he takes his mom's advice and signs up to art classes.

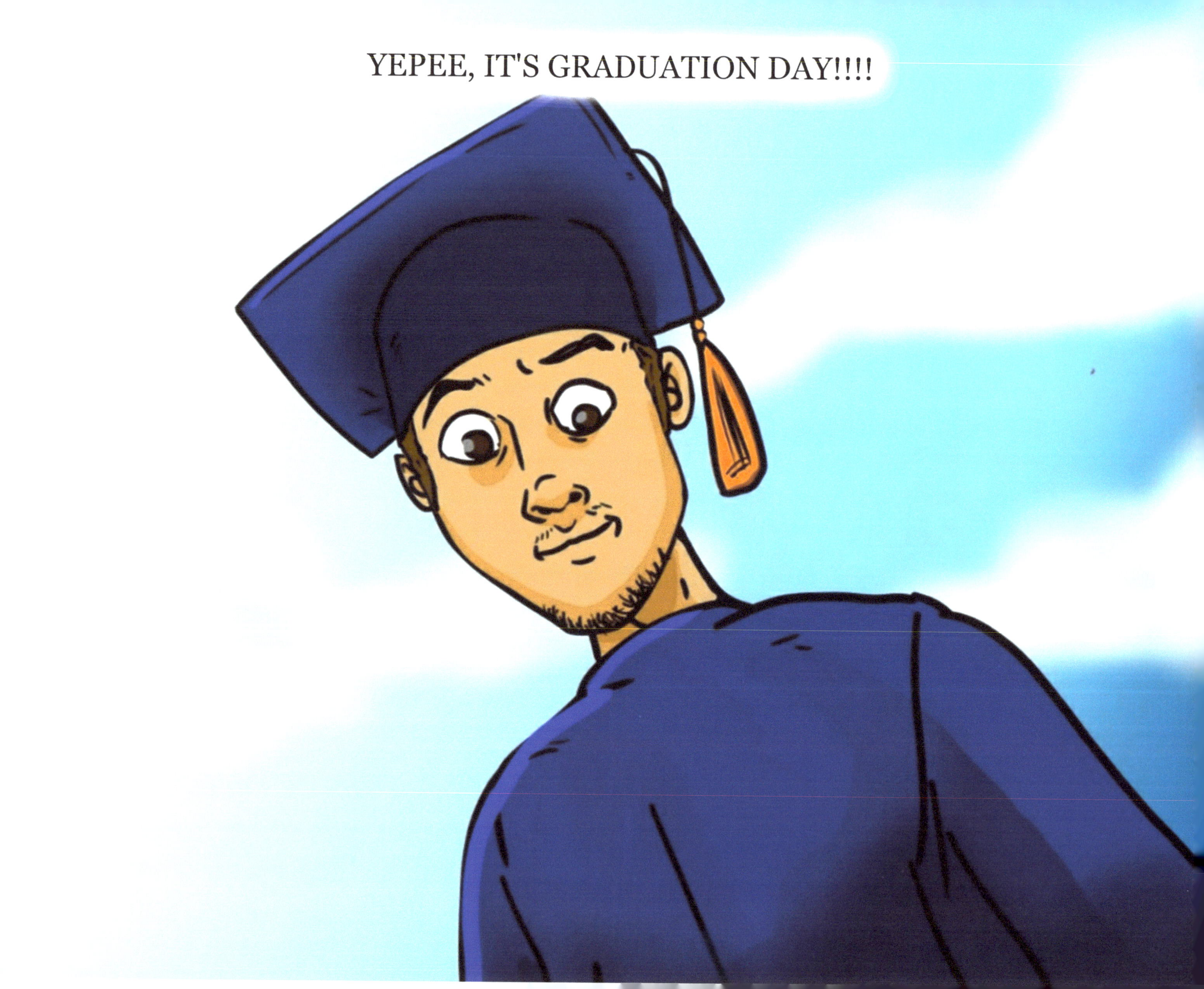
YEPEE, IT'S GRADUATION DAY!!!!

Years later, Eugene begins to attend church at Word of Faith Church

International. he remembers the Sunday morning that Pastor, Dr. Rick V. Layton stops in the middle of his sermon and asks for him to come in front of the church. It was there that Dr. Layton spoke these worlds, "God is going to make your name great and people all over the world will know your name. In Jesus' name!" Eugene's life will never be same again.

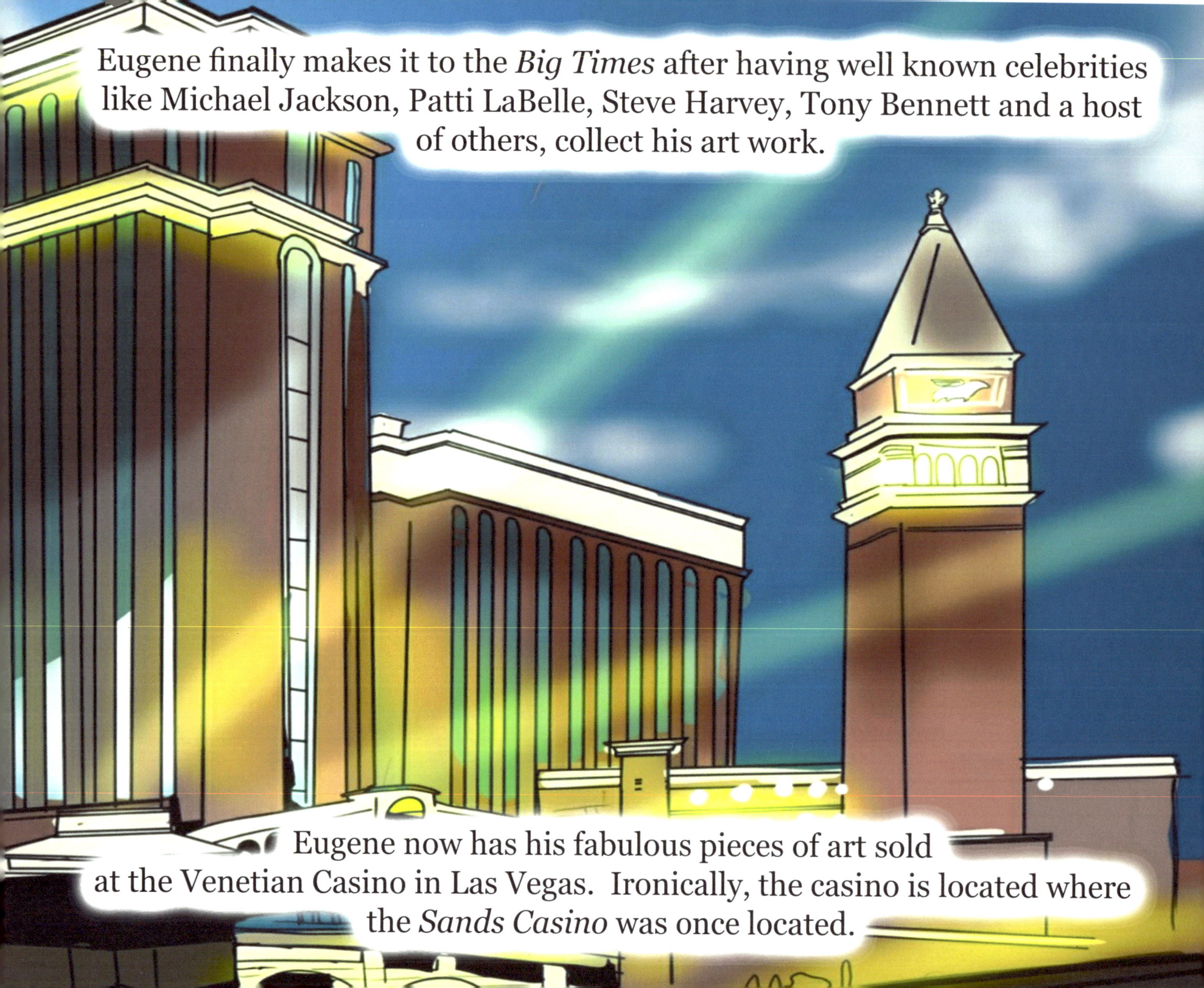

One day, while Eugene was doing an art demonstration at the world famous Regis Galerie located inside the Venetian Casino, he notices a kid who had walked in with his parents, admiring his art work. Eugene could tell he wanted to see what all the people were looking at.

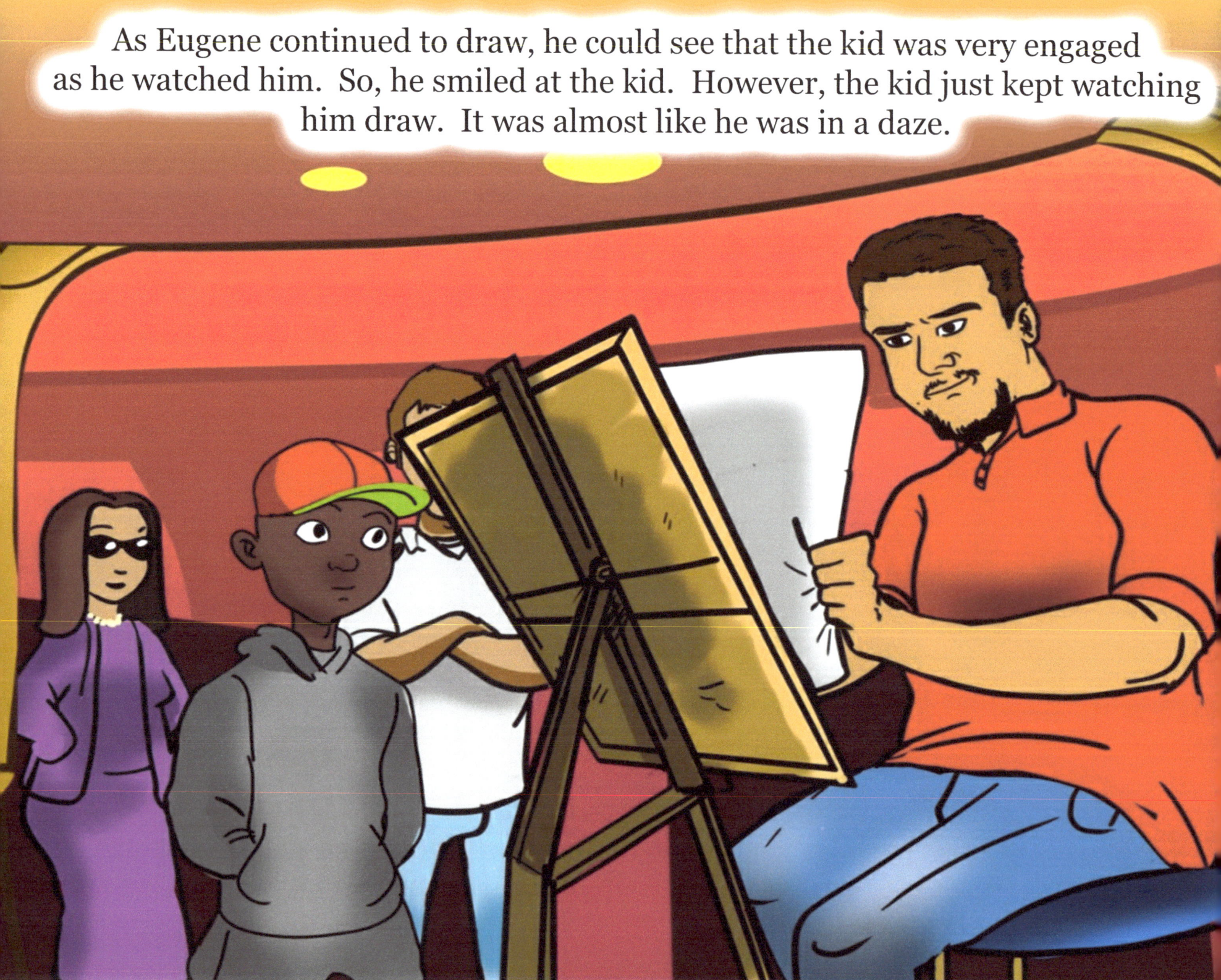

As time went on, the kid did not leave. It was time for Eugene to meet his fans. The kid was right there and Eugene asked him "What is your name young man?" The kid said his name was Christ. "Hi, Christ!" Eugene said with a smile on his face as he was autographing a small postcard. When Eugene finished, he called

out and said, "Hey, Chris", here. This is for you. Chris said, "Is this for me?" Yes, Chris it is just for you. With an excited voice, young Chris says, "I know what I want to be when I grow up!"

Now, Eugene is a grown man and no more Greyhound bus trips. He has moved up to private jets and big planes as he travels the world!

On September 15, 2020, the city of Shreveport, Louisiana honored Eugene with a street sign dedication in the 3800 block of Mayfield Street with his name "Eugene Mosley."

"CHAIRMAN OF THE BOARD"

Tony Bennett

The Eugene Mosley Story

Duke Ellington	Frank Sinatra	Sands Casino	Walk of Stars
Steve Harvey	Pointillism	Regis Galerie	Kim Waters
Greyhound	Dean Martin	Sammy Davis	Jazz Music
Southwood	Las Vegas	Grandma	Artist

Special Thanks

I would like to give thanks to God for giving me this talent that I have.

A special thanks to The Mosley family for sticking by me and telling me to never give up, I love you with all of my heart.

The Frazier Family for all the love and prayers, I love you.

The Rambo family, Las Vegas for taking such great care of me when I was young and living in Vegas, I love you.

Mr. Kim Waters, thank you so much my brother for narrating the book, producing and performing the great soundtracks and being a great friend for all these years.

Mr. Ron Johnson, thank you so much.

Mr. Steve Harvey, a true friend, you the man.

Ms. Pattie Labelle. You are such a wonderful person. I thank you for believing in me when I first started my career.

The Regis Gallerie in Las Vegas, Nevada.

The Las Vegas Walk of Stars and the State of Nevada.

The City of Shreveport, Louisiana.

The Northwest Louisiana Walk of Stars and Lieutenant Governor, Mr. Billy Nungesser and the State of Louisiana.

Legacy One International

Special Thanks Continued

Personal Chef, Stanley Saint Charles; I wish you much success and "thank you" for being a friend and one of the best chefs along with many others that I know.

The great people and my fans of the Philippines, Scotland, The United Kingdom, Dubai, France, and Germany, "thank you."

Dr. Rick V. Layton for giving me the great and powerful word of God in my life. I will never forget you and The Refreshing Point Ministries Family.

Anthony Francis.

Mr. Billy Adger and his wonderful family.

My Agents, Mr. Bench M. Bello & Mr. Barrett Laroda.

Ms. Khalilah Camacho Ali, Mr. Jerome Thomas, and to all the kids around the world, always dream BIG and never, ever, give up on your dreams.

Special thanks to Shreveport City Councilman James Green.

Thank you, The Barnes Family of Malcom Explains, for seeing my vision, thank you.

"And, look out Hollywood California Walk of Fame, I'm coming!"

www.ingramcontent.com/pod-product-compliance
Lightning Source LLC
Chambersburg PA
CBHW041108210426

43209CB00063BA/1851